COURTNEY CARBONE

THE
LAUGH-OUT-LOUD,
JUST-SLIGHTLY-EMBARRASSING
BOOK OF TRUTH OR DARE

WORKMAN PUBLISHING, NEW YORK

Library of Congress Cataloging-in-Publication Data is available.

ISBN 978-1-5235-0476-3

Design by Jooahn Kwon

Workman books are available at special discounts when purchased in bulk for premiums and sales promotions as well as for fund-raising or educational use. Special editions or book excerpts can also be created to specification. For details, contact the Special Sales Director at the address below, or send an email to specialmarkets@workman.com.

Workman Publishing Co., Inc.
225 Varick Street
New York, NY 10014-4381
workman.com

Workman is a registered trademark of Workman Publishing Co., Inc.

Printed in Canada
First printing September 2019

10 9 8 7 6 5 4 3 2 1

Are you ready to play Truth or Dare?

How to Play:

Find a friend or family member who wants to play. Open the book to any page and ask your partner, "Truth or Dare?" If they say "Truth," read them the question from the left page. If they say "Dare," challenge them to complete the action on the right page. Then switch, and let them ask you a Truth or Dare!

Some Ground Rules:

1. Safety first! Don't *smell*, *eat*, or *do* anything that isn't safe, or that you or a friend might be allergic to. (If you are unsure if something is safe, ask a parent or guardian.)

2. Don't pressure someone to say or do something they aren't comfortable with. Just choose a different page instead.

3. If someone tells you a secret while playing the game, don't blab to everyone at school the next day. No one likes that kid!

4. Be aware of your surroundings so you don't accidentally knock over a priceless vase or sprain your ankle while practicing your zombie walk.

5. Don't worry about looking silly. The whole point of the game is to have fun!

Disclaimer:

Use common sense when doing the dares! Neither the author nor the publisher shall be liable for any damage that may be caused or sustained as a result of conducting the activities in this book, so be careful when tap dancing, stomping on all fours like an elephant, and sneaking around your house like a ninja.

Let the games begin!

TRUTH

Do you sing in the shower?

DID YOU KNOW?

Americans use more than one trillion gallons of water showering each year. That's enough water to fill more than 1,500,000 Olympic-size swimming pools!

COVER YOUR EARS!

It is possible for a singer to hit a note high enough to break glass—but the note would have to be 100 decibels or more!

DARE

SING a line of your favorite song as **LOUD** as you can.

A-CHOO!

Contrary to popular belief, sneezing with your eyes open will NOT make your eyeballs pop out!

TRUTH

Have you ever sneezed on someone?

DARE

Fake a loud ~~sneeze~~ in public.

Are you allergic to the sun? About one in four people sneeze in response to bright light. This reaction is known as photic sneeze reflex.

TRUTH

Have you ever had a crush on a fictional character?

Q. Why was Cupid in the hospital?

A. He was love*sick*.

Q. What do drivers listen to on the radio?

A. Car-*tunes*.

DARE

Talk like your favorite CARTOON CHARACTER for the next five minutes.

TRUTH

Who is your favorite celebrity?

DARE

Act out a scene from your favorite movie playing *ALL* the characters!

The first full-length movies with sound premiered in the 1920s, and were called "talkies."

TRUTH

Do you ever sleep with stuffed animals?

FUN FACT

The teddy bear gets its name from President Theodore "Teddy" Roosevelt.

DID YOU KNOW?

Some people have a medical condition that makes them eat while they sleep.

DARE

Pretend to SLEEPWALK around your home—and see how long you can keep up the ruse!

Q. Why was the boy arguing
   with his invisible friend?
A. They couldn't see eye
   to eye.

TRUTH

*Do you, or did you
ever, have an invisible
friend?*

DARE

Don't say ANYTHING at all for the next five minutes.

Q. Why was the mouse so quiet?

A. The cat got his tongue.

TRUTH

How much time do you spend staring at a computer or phone each day?

DID YOU KNOW?

One of the most popular internet passwords is "123456," followed by—you guessed it— the word "password"!

SIGN ME UP!

You can earn a degree in yodeling from Lucerne University of Applied Sciences and Arts in Switzerland.

DARE

Yodel for one full minute.

TRUTH

Do you ever dance when no one is around?

DARE

Do a **FUNKY DANCE** for thirty seconds.

Q. Why do dancers like to freestyle?

A. Because it doesn't cost them anything.

TRUTH

What's your middle name?

DID YOU KNOW?

Many celebrities, like Reese Witherspoon and Meghan Markle, use their middle names as their first or last names. Others, like Lady Gaga and Bruno Mars, use stage names that are completely different from their real names.

TWIN TROUBLE

Two sets of identical twins in Bogotá, Colombia, were switched at birth, and no one realized until decades later. Eventually, all four young men met each other and figured out the mix-up, thanks to the help of two friends who noticed their physical similarities.

DARE

SWITCH NAMES with a friend for the rest of the day.

Q. Why was the dentist studying?

A. He wanted to *brush up* on his skills.

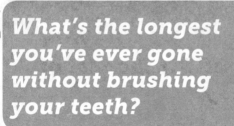

TRUTH

What's the longest you've ever gone without brushing your teeth?

DARE

BRUSH *your teeth with the hand you don't usually use.*

Q. Why did the dentist run to work?

A. She was in a tooth-*rush*!

TRUTH

Has a bird ever pooped on you?

DID YOU KNOW?

Bird poop, also known as guano, might seem gross to us humans, but plants love it! Guano is often used as fertilizer.

Q. What kind of stamp doesn't cost anything?

A. A stamp of approval!

DARE

Write a letter to your future self.

When you outgrow your old clothes, don't throw them away! Donate them to a good cause or repurpose them. Textile recyclers can turn unusable clothing into wiping rags or insulation.

TRUTH

How old is your oldest piece of clothing?

DARE

Show everyone the holey-est pair of socks in your drawer.

To "darn" something means to mend it by stitching it back together.

TRUTH

Do your feet ever get really smelly?

Q. Why wasn't the shoemaker nervous about getting the job?

A. She was a *shoe*-in!

STINK-BE-GONE!

Crinkled-up newspaper pages can absorb bad household odors.

DARE

Take a whiff of the STINKIEST shoes in the house.

TRUTH

Have you ever gotten gum stuck in your hair?

DARE

Let a friend style your hair **HOWEVER** they want. (But no cutting!)

Q. Why did the rabbit go to the salon?

A. He needed a *hare*-cut!

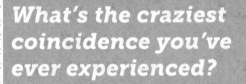

TRUTH

What's the craziest coincidence you've ever experienced?

WAIT A SECOND . . .

Déjà vu is the feeling that you've seen or heard something before. For example, *déjà vu* is the feeling that you've seen or heard something before.

Q. Why was the piece of paper
nervous for tryouts?

A. He didn't want to get *cut*.

DARE

**Write your name on a
piece of paper WITHOUT
using your hands.**

(*Tip: Try holding the pen between your toes!*)

TRUTH

Have you ever stayed up all night long?

DARE

BUILD a pillow fort and sleep inside it tonight.

Q. Why didn't the pillow want anything for dinner?

A. It was already *stuffed*!

TRUTH

Have you ever accidentally drunk expired milk?

DID YOU KNOW?

Most foods shouldn't be moldy, but that's not necessarily true for all cheeses. Certain types of mold are actually used to make Brie and blue cheese. (But as a general rule, if food is moldy, stay away!)

Q. Why did the milk carton always get his way?

A. He was *spoiled*.

DARE

Eat a bowl of cereal with *WATER* instead of milk.

Q. What did the gym teacher say when he got to the locker room?

A. "Home, *sweat* home!"

TRUTH

Have you ever sweat through your clothes?

DARE

Pretend you're a frog and jump as HIGH as you can!

HOW MANY?!

There are more than 4,000 species of frogs . . . and that doesn't include the kind that gets stuck in your throat!

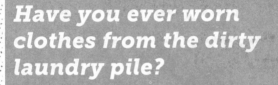

TRUTH

Have you ever worn clothes from the dirty laundry pile?

DID YOU KNOW?

Before there were washers and dryers, people used devices called "washboards" to help them clean clothes. The boards were covered in ridges, which also meant they could be scratched up and down to make music!

SCORE!

Baskets aren't just good for holding laundry. When the sport of basketball was invented, it was originally played with peach baskets instead of nets!

DARE

Wear something from the DIRTY laundry basket for the next hour.

TRUTH

What's the spiciest thing you've ever eaten?

DARE

Try to *TAP* dance.

Have you ever heard of *soft shoe*? It's a type of tap dancing that involves tapping and sliding your feet using shoes without metal taps.

TRUTH

Have you ever taken a really awful selfie?

CAMERA MAGIC

If you turn your phone or video camera upside down and record yourself lying flat on the floor, the final video will look like you're on the ceiling!

DARE

Take a *silly* selfie and show your friends.

DID YOU KNOW?

Researchers at a university in England believe urine can power electricity.

TRUTH

Have you ever peed in the shower?

DARE

Draw a picture of your crush . . . then see if your friends can guess who it is!

Before people could take pictures, they hired artists to do professional portraits. The artists knew that people like to look good, so the portraits might have been more flattering than realistic!

TRUTH

How many baby teeth do you still have?

Q. What did the orthodontist say to her patient?

A. *"Brace* yourself!"

DARE

Show your friends a baby picture of you.

TRUTH

What's the longest you've ever gone without changing your underwear?

DARE

Wear a pair of underwear *INSIDE OUT* for a whole day.

A boy named Jack Singer holds the record for the most pairs of underwear worn at one time—215 pairs!

TRUTH

Have you ever left a really embarrassing phone message you wanted to take back?

DID YOU KNOW?

There are telephones shaped like hamburgers! (French fries not included.)

CAN YOU HEAR ME?

How did humans quickly send messages over long distances before the telephone or email? Throughout history, people have used lots of creative methods to get their messages across, including smoke, light, and flag signals.

DARE

Text a friend a *silly* joke.

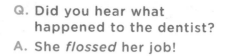

Q. Did you hear what happened to the dentist?

A. She *flossed* her job!

TRUTH

Do you floss your teeth?

DARE

Play musical chairs with friends, _SINGING_ all the songs yourself.

Q. Why did the opera singer quit during the middle of a show?

A. He wanted to go out on a _high note_.

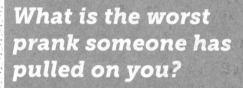

TRUTH

What is the worst prank someone has pulled on you?

NOT-SO-FUN FACT

A stinky trick some pranksters play around Halloween is covering onions in caramel sauce and pretending they are caramel apples. Gross!

One of the most famous beds in history is a giant four-poster bed called the "Great Bed of Ware" in England. Built around the year 1590, the bed is over 10 feet wide and 11 feet long!

DARE

Make your bed
upside down.

DID YOU KNOW?

The giant armadillo wins the award for mammal with the most teeth—these critters have up to 100 chompers!

TRUTH

Have you ever accidentally used someone else's toothbrush?

58

DARE

Do an impression of a *RADIO* announcer.

Q. Why were the peas at the radio station?

A. They were recording a *pod*-cast.

TRUTH

What's something no one knows about you?

WHAT'S YOUR TYPE?

While there are many different types of blood, the eight most common ones are A+, A-, B+, B-, AB+, AB-, O+, and O-.

Q. What is a ninja's favorite food?

A. *Sword*-fish.

DARE

Sneak around your house like a ninja for five minutes.

Q. What was the car
   dealership's store policy?
A. "You *brake* it, you buy it!"

TRUTH

*Have you ever knocked
over a display in a
store?*

DARE

Wear sunglasses *upside down* for the next hour.

COOL SHADES

Elton John is famous for his music . . . and his sunglasses! The beloved singer has worn a variety of outlandish sunglasses throughout his career.

TRUTH

Have you ever peed in someone's pool?

MYTHBUSTER

Ever heard that if you pee in a pool, the water will change color? This is a myth!

While werewolves aren't real outside of folklore, some people have a medical condition known as clinical lycanthropy that causes them to believe they are wolves.

DARE

Pretend to transform into a WEREWOLF.

TRUTH

Do you have any birthmarks?

DARE

Pretend to play a harmonica—and try to MIMIC the instrument's sound!

A woman in Switzerland holds the record for longest amount of time continuously playing the harmonica— 24 hours!

TRUTH

Are you allergic to anything?

DOG DILEMMA

While some dogs may cause allergy sufferers less trouble, there really is no such thing as a 100% hypoallergenic (allergy-free) dog.

DARE

Give a friend a FOOT massage.

TRUTH

Do you use mouthwash?

DARE

"Swim" around the room like a SHARK. Don't forget your fin!

Shark attacks are scary, but fatal ones are actually very rare. Only about 5 to 10 people are killed by shark attacks each year.

TRUTH

Have you ever fallen off your chair?

JUST DON'T POKE A HOLE!

Not all furniture is made from heavy, sturdy materials. In fact, inflatable furniture—which is filled entirely of air—is just the opposite! (The upside is that it's easy to move.)

Need to confirm the spelling of something? Use the "NATO phonetic alphabet," a set of 26 code words that help identify individual letters. Some of the code words are "Alfa," "Bravo," "Charlie," and "Delta."

DARE

Create a code **name for your crush.**

TRUTH

What is the grossest thing you've ever eaten?

DARE

Write a SONG about your crush—and sing it out loud!

A song sung without musical accompaniment is performed "a cappella."

TRUTH

Have you ever been stung by a bee?

Q. What kind of haircut did the bee get?

A. A *buzz* cut!

An American man holds the record for most underwater jump rope jumps in a single hour—1,608. (He had to wear scuba gear, of course!)

DARE

Stage a *JUMP ROPE* competition with your friends. If you don't have jump ropes, just pretend you do!

TRUTH

Where were you born?

DARE

Screech and **flap**
your arms like a bat.

Bracken Cave
in Texas is home
to 15 million bats,
making it the world's
largest bat colony.

TRUTH

What kind of pajamas do you wear?

Q. What do medieval warriors wear to bed?

A. *Knight*-gowns.

DEEP BREATH

Meditation is a practice that can be used to improve overall health and well-being. Often it involves focusing on your breath, which can help you get in touch with the present moment.

DARE

Sit on the floor, close your eyes, and try to meditate for one minute.

Q. Is a booger the same thing as mucus?

A. No, it's *snot*.

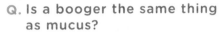

TRUTH

Do you ever pick your nose?

DARE

Read out loud the LAST three text messages you sent.

THAT'S EASY!

Feeling peckish, but don't like talking on the phone? Fear not! There's now a service that lets you order a pizza by just texting.

TRUTH

What is your biggest goal in life?

DREAM BIG

Many performers dream of one day achieving an "EGOT." This rare accomplishment means winning one each of the following awards: an Emmy (for television), a Grammy (for music), an Oscar (for film), and a Tony (for theater).

DID YOU KNOW?

Eyeliner was popular in ancient Egypt! In fact, when King Tut's tomb was excavated in the 1920s, the famous boy king had dark makeup around his eyes.

DARE

Let your friends give you a MAKEOVER.

TRUTH

Have you ever broken something valuable?

DARE

Pretend you are _queen_ or _king_ for the day.

Does a day
not seem like
enough time
to be in charge?
How about a month?
William Henry Harrison
only served as president
of the United States for
one month before he died!

TRUTH

Have you ever kept something that you borrowed?

DID YOU KNOW?

Ever heard the phrase "possession is nine-tenths of the law"? This means that once someone has something (even if it doesn't belong to them), it's very difficult for the original owner to get it back.

FUN FACT

The record for most people playing kazoo at one time is 5,190, set in the UK in 2011.

DARE

PRETEND to play a kazoo.

YUM!

There are more than 1,900 species of edible insects, including ants, beetles, and grasshoppers!

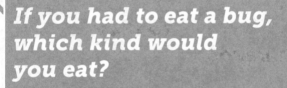

TRUTH

If you had to eat a bug, which kind would you eat?

DARE

GUESS *your and your crush's future professions.*

Looking for an unusual profession? You could become a dog-surfing instructor! (Yes, that's a real thing!)

TRUTH

Have you ever peed in the ocean?

PLUG YOUR NOSE!

On cruise ships, the waste from toilets and urinals is called "blackwater." While blackwater is allowed to be dumped into the ocean, there are many rules about where and how (for example, it can't be dumped too close to land).

Q. Why was the magician so good at card tricks?

A. He was a real *ace*!

DARE

Pretend to be a magician and make something disappear

TRUTH

Have you ever fixed a wedgie in public?

DARE

Put on as many pairs of socks as you can at once.

No socks for Albert Einstein! In a letter he wrote, the genius physicist complained that his big toe kept making holes in his socks, so he stopped wearing them.

TRUTH

What is your biggest fear?

WHERE IS FLOOR 13?

Triskaidekaphobia is the fear of the number 13. This fear is so prevalent that many tall buildings are designed without a 13th floor!

AND MY WIFE WILL BE . . .

Long ago in New England, people peeled apples in one long strip and threw the peel over their shoulder. They believed that whatever letter shape the peel made when it landed was the first letter of their future match's name.

DARE

GUESS *the crush of one of your friends. You get three tries!*

TRUTH

What three things would you want if you were trapped on a desert island?

DARE

ROAR like a lion.

Q. What game do lion cubs like to play?

A. *Pride*-and-seek.

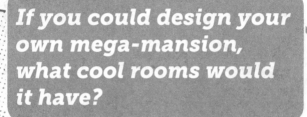

TRUTH

If you could design your own mega-mansion, what cool rooms would it have?

CAN WE TRADE HOMES?

A lakefront mega-mansion designed for NBA legend Shaquille O'Neal has its own recording studio, dance studio, movie theater, 17-car garage, and—you guessed it—an indoor basketball court!

When people lie, their heart rate and blood pressure often increase and they may begin to sweat. Lie detectors measure these tell-tale signs—but the jury is out on whether lie detectors actually work.

DARE

Play Two Truths and a Lie with a friend. Tell your friend two real facts and one lie about yourself. See if they can guess which is the lie!

Q. Why did the nose want to shower?

A. It *smelled*.

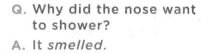

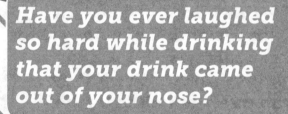

TRUTH

Have you ever laughed so hard while drinking that your drink came out of your nose?

DARE

Pretend you are a thirsty VAMPIRE out for blood.

FACT OR FICTION?

Ever heard of Transylvania? It's a place often associated with Dracula, a famous literary vampire. But while bloodsucking vampires aren't real, Transylvania is! It's a region in Romania.

TRUTH

Have you ever farted in public?

DID YOU KNOW?

Want to impress your friends with a fancy word for farts? Try "flatulence." But be warned, this word also means talking in a pompous or arrogant way . . . like trying to use an overly fancy word for farts!

Q. Why was the actor asked to leave the movie set?

A. He was making a *scene*.

DARE

Pretend to be a FAMOUS MOVIE STAR at a red-carpet premiere.

Q. Why wasn't the mirror ready to be sold?

A. It needed more time to *reflect*.

TRUTH

Do you ever talk to yourself in the mirror?

DARE

Pretend the ground is LAVA and get from one side of the room to the other without touching the floor!

VOLCANOES IN SPACE!

Io, one of the moons of Jupiter, has more volcanic activity than any other planet or moon in our solar system.

TRUTH

How long does it take you to get ready in the morning?

FUN FACT

The woman with the world's longest hair has a mane that's over 18 feet long! Imagine having to brush *that* out every day.

X MARKS THE SPOT

In 2018, a buried treasure lost at sea for hundreds of years was found in the Caribbean. The treasure, which included gold, silver, and emeralds, could be worth as much as 17 *billion* dollars!

DARE

Pretend you just found buried *TREASURE*.

PARROT BOOGIE

You probably know that parrots can imitate human speech, but did you know that parrots have also been observed dancing to human music?

TRUTH

Do you ever talk to animals?

DARE

SING a song you know, but change all of the words to make it about something totally different.

Did you ever notice that the "Alphabet Song," "Twinkle, Twinkle, Little Star," and "Baa, Baa, Black Sheep" all have the same tune? Think about it!

TRUTH

Are you scared of spiders or creepy crawlers?

DID YOU KNOW?

Unlike many spiders, tarantulas don't need to use webs to catch their prey. Instead, they inject venom into their victims to paralyze them.

Q. What happened to the sketch artist?

A. She vanished without a *trace*!

DARE

Pretend to PAINT a large wall mural.

DID YOU KNOW?

Certain types of flowers are edible. In fact, many bakers and chefs use edible flowers to make their dishes, salads, and cakes more colorful. (But don't try eating flowers at home!)

TRUTH

Have you ever given anyone flowers?

DARE

FLOP around like a fish out of water.

Q. Why didn't the fisherman catch anything?

A. He was just fishing for compliments.

TRUTH

Have you ever accidentally downloaded a computer virus?

NOT-SO-FUN FACT

In the year 2000, millions of people accidentally downloaded the "I LOVE YOU" computer virus, thinking it was a love letter!

Q. Where did the TV go for vacation?

A. To a *remote* island.

DARE

HUM a TV theme song from start to finish. Ask your friends to guess the show!

TRUTH

Are you superstitious?

DARE

Let a friend give you *"FACIAL HAIR"* using whipped cream or shaving cream.

A handlebar mustache is so-named because it resembles the handlebars of a bicycle. Many historical figures sported this distinctive look, including President William Howard Taft.

TRUTH

Have you ever pretended to be someone else on the phone?

SECRET SOUNDS

There are certain high-pitched ringtones that most adults can't hear.

DARE

Act like there is an INVISIBLE mosquito buzzing around your face.

TRUTH

What is the scariest movie you've ever seen?

DID YOU KNOW?

The Motion Picture Association of America has been rating films for over 50 years.

BZZZZ

During the 1960s, there was a popular hairstyle known as a "beehive" because it . . . wait for it . . . looked like a beehive!

DARE

Show everyone a picture of the WORST HAIRCUT you've ever gotten.

TRUTH

What do you daydream about most?

DID YOU KNOW?

There is a real island in Australia called Daydream Island.

DROP A BEAT!

When someone *beatboxes*, they imitate the sounds of a drum machine with their mouth and voice.

DARE

Try to **BEATBOX** while a friend sings.

TRUTH

Do you believe in ghosts?

DARE

Try to dance like a BALLERINA.

Q. Why did
the ballerina
practice so
hard?

A. The *barre* was set
very high.

Q. Why was the firefly so impatient?

A. It couldn't wait to *glow* up!

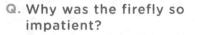

TRUTH

Are you scared of the dark?

DARE

Create your own card or board game and challenge your friends to play. The SILLIER, the better!

DID YOU KNOW?

During World War II, Allied troops used Monopoly board game boxes to smuggle real money and escape maps to prisoners of war who had been captured by the Nazis.

Q. Why was the astronaut so relaxed at the awards show?

A. She was used to being around *stars*.

TRUTH

Who is the most famous person you've ever met?

DARE

Show everyone the _LAST_ picture you took with your phone or camera.

Q. Why didn't anyone like the new camera?

A. It was too *flash*-y.

TRUTH

What is your bedtime?

Q. What household object is ambidextrous?

A. A clock—it uses *both hands*!

132

Q. Why wasn't the snake able to hiss?

A. He was *tongue*-tied!

DARE

Try to curl your TONGUE into a circle shape.

Q. Why was the candymaker all dressed up?

A. She was going to a gum-*ball*!

TRUTH

Have you ever eaten so much candy that you got a stomachache?

DARE

Wear a HALLOWEEN costume for the rest of the day.

FUN FACT

When candy corn was first invented, the manufacturer called it "Chicken Feed." It was sold in packages with a rooster on the front of the box.

TRUTH

What are you most scared of: lions, tigers, or bears?

DID YOU KNOW?

If you live in the US, you're not likely to see a lion or a tiger unless you're at a zoo or wildlife sanctuary. Bears, on the other hand, do roam freely in some parts of the country.

KEEP IT SNAPPY

A Japanese university student named Satoyuki Fujimura currently holds the world record for most finger snaps in one minute: 296!

DARE

SNAP *your fingers for a full minute straight.*

Some furniture manufacturers produce bookcases, tables, and bed frames with "secret" compartments for holding valuables—or anything else you don't want out in the open.

TRUTH

What is the most embarrassing thing you own?

DARE

Pretend you are driving AN IMAGINARY CAR and stop to pick up your friends one at a time.

If you could somehow drive straight from Earth to the moon at 60 mph, it would take you just under six months.

TRUTH

Have you ever sat in something that left a stain on your pants?

YUCK!

Watch out for dung beetles! Not surprisingly, these beetles are named because of their tendency to eat the "dung" (poop) of other animals.

Q. What did the goat say to her friend?

A. "Have you *herd* the news?"

DARE

BLEAT *like a goat.*

There is a kind of soda that is bacon flavored.

TRUTH

What is the grossest thing you've ever drunk?

DARE

Challenge a friend to a TASTE TEST. No peeking!
(And nothing your friend might be allergic to!)

Q. Why did the bake-off judge bring a friend?

A. They were *taste buds*!

TRUTH

What is the last thing that made you cry?

NOT-SO-FUN FACT

Onions make humans cry because they contain an eye irritant that gets released during cutting.

ZZZZZ

You might think newborns spend most of their time crying—but in reality, they sleep about 16 to 18 hours a day!

DARE

Wail like a newborn baby.

TRAITOR!

During the Revolutionary War, Benedict Arnold served as a military officer for the Americans—before switching sides to help the British. To call someone a "Benedict Arnold" is to call them a traitor.

TRUTH

Have you ever spied on anyone?

DARE

Do a **FREESTYLE RAP** for two minutes.

Q. What is a hip-hop star's favorite sandwich?

A. A *rap*!

TRUTH

Have you ever forgotten your own name?

DID YOU KNOW?

While people with amnesia may have trouble learning new information or remembering past events, they don't usually forget who they are.

FUN FACT

Spelling your name backward is easy when it's a "palindrome," a word that is spelled the same backward and forward (for example, "Anna" or "Otto").

DARE

Spell your name BACKWARD without messing up. Bonus points if you do your full name!

Q. What animals sleep the most?

A. *Zzz*-ebras!

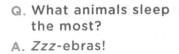

TRUTH

Do you talk in your sleep?

DARE

Call a friend and SING them a song.

Q. Why did the conductor turn his back on the audience?

A. It was time to face the music.

TRUTH

Have you ever sent someone a secret note?

DID YOU KNOW?

In total, Americans purchase about 7 *billion* greeting cards each year.

DON'T EAT IT!

The Prince of Wales once received a message inscribed on a single grain of rice.

DARE

Write a message to a friend using the smallest handwriting **possible. See if they can read it!**

TRUTH

Are you scared of small spaces?

DARE

Use your own closet to CREATE A FASHION SHOW.

Q. Why were the fashion designers such good friends?

A. They had *sew* much in common.

TRUTH

Have you ever called someone the wrong name?

WHO SAID THAT?

During the 86th Academy Awards, actor John Travolta mistakenly introduced singer Idina Menzel by the wrong name in front of millions of viewers. But it didn't end there! A year later, Idina turned the tables when she jokingly introduced John by the wrong name.

In an interview, Kate Winslet said she keeps her Best Actress Oscar trophy in her bathroom. Why? So that guests can make pretend acceptance speeches in the mirror!

DARE

Give an *ACCEPTANCE SPEECH* for an award.

TRUTH

Have you ever had any cavities?

DARE

Talk like a *PIRATE* for the next five minutes.

The front of a boat is called the "bow." The back of the boat is called the "stern." The left side of a boat is called "port." The right side of a boat is called "starboard."

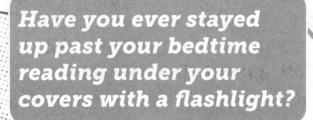

TRUTH

Have you ever stayed up past your bedtime reading under your covers with a flashlight?

Q. Why did the girl stay in bed on career day?

A. She wanted to become an *undercover* agent.

ROYAL FLUSH

Playing cards have been around since the 1300s, but they were initially hand-painted and were too expensive for most people to own.

DARE

Build a card castle as **HIGH** *as you can.*

BE CAREFUL!

Picking your nose can cause a nosebleed!

TRUTH

Have you ever had a nosebleed?

DARE

Try singing **OPERA**.

Florence, Italy,
is considered the
birthplace of opera.

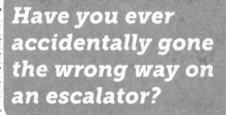

TRUTH

Have you ever accidentally gone the wrong way on an escalator?

DID YOU KNOW?

Some escalators have motion sensors and only run when people need them.

SIGNED, SEALED, DELIVERED

You can buy stamps specifically made for postcards, and they actually cost less than letter stamps.

DARE

Make a postcard from a FICTIONAL PLACE and send it to a friend.

If someone is named Nick, is their real name also their nickname?

TRUTH

What is your least favorite nickname?

DARE

Bark like a SEA LION and walk around the room on your "flippers."

Is it a sea lion or a seal? If the animal is making a lot of noise and surrounded by friends, it's probably a sea lion. Seals, on the other hand, tend to be quieter and more solitary.

TRUTH

Have you ever been on TV, on the radio, or featured in a newspaper?

Q. How did the cat get on the TV?

A. He was a very good climber.

WHO SAID THAT?

Ventriloquists are able to "throw" their voices to make it sound like the voice is coming from somewhere—or someone—else (often a puppet). This stagecraft goes all the way back to ancient Greece!

DARE

Try to talk WITHOUT moving your mouth.

Pet hedgehogs like to play with cardboard toilet paper tubes. This form of play is so popular that it actually has a name: "tubing." But because hedgehogs can get their heads stuck in the tubes, they often need help to free themselves.

TRUTH

Have you ever run out of toilet paper at a really bad time?

DARE

Challenge someone to a *THUMB WAR*.

Speaking of thumbs, the world's smallest horse, Thumbelina, is 17.5 inches tall and weighs about 57 pounds! At this size, the miniature mare is smaller than many household dogs.

TRUTH

Have you ever stepped in gum?

DID YOU KNOW?

In California, you can visit Bubblegum Alley, where the alleyway walls are covered in chewed bubble gum.

DARE

Pretend to blow a _GIANT_ bubble gum bubble.

TRUTH

Do you know your crush's phone number by heart?

DARE

Sing a _HEARTFELT LULLABY_ to an object in the room.

Lullabies have been around for a _long_ time. In fact, the lyrics of a lullaby were discovered on an ancient Babylonian clay tablet dating to 2,000 BC!

TRUTH

Do you lick the bowl when baking?

NOT-SO-FUN FACT

People who consume raw eggs—like those in cookie dough—can end up getting sick with salmonella.

While most owls are nocturnal, the snowy owl does most of its hunting during the day. And despite its wintry name, it's actually busiest during summertime!

DARE

HOOT and turn your head like an owl.

Q. Which animals are the most affectionate?

A. *Love*-birds!

TRUTH

Have you ever accidentally said "I love you" to someone?

DARE

Create your own DANCE ROUTINE.

Q. Why was the runner such a good singer?

A. He never forgot a *track*.

TRUTH

Have you ever failed a test or quiz?

DID YOU KNOW?

Cha Sa-soon, a South Korean woman, took—and failed—her driving test hundreds of times. Finally, on her 960th attempt, she passed! She is now a local celebrity.

YOU'VE EARNED IT!

There are lots of stores that will give students freebies (like free pizza, doughnuts, or ice cream) for having a good report card.

DARE

Show someone your last REPORT CARD.

TRUTH

Are you scared of germs?

DARE

Talk in a really DEEP VOICE.

Q. Why did the balloon sound so funny?

A. He was full of helium!

TRUTH

What celebrity do people think you look like most?

FUN FACT

Some celebrity look-alikes make impersonating celebs into a career!

184

Late-night shows are usually taped earlier in the day and then aired at night.

DARE

Pretend you are a late-night television host and INTERVIEW A FRIEND.

Q. What is a farmer's favorite salad dressing?

A. *Ranch.*

TRUTH

Do you double-dip when eating chips or fries?

DARE

Try to HYPN⊙TIZE a friend.

LOOK INTO MY EYES . . .

Despite what you may have seen on TV or in movies, people can't be hypnotized against their will.

TRUTH

What was your most embarrassing moment playing a sport?

DID YOU KNOW?

Michael Jordan, widely considered one of the best basketball players of all time, did not make his high school varsity basketball team the first time he tried out. With hard work and persistence, he made the varsity team the following year.

Q. What advice do they give pilots in flight school?

A. "If at first you don't succeed, fly, fly again!"

DARE

Stand on ONE FOOT for the next thirty seconds.

I'LL BE IN MY POD

Do you remember naptime fondly? Then you might be interested to know that some workplaces actually offer "nap pods" for sleepy employees.

TRUTH

Have you ever fallen asleep at school?

DARE

Laugh like a *HYENA*.

Hyenas are carnivorous scavengers who eat dead and decaying animals.

TRUTH

Do you always wash your hands after using the bathroom?

FUN FACT

Stool is another word for "poop."

Ever heard of an Axel, Salchow, or a Lutz in figure skating? These jumps are all named after the people who created them.

DARE

Act like an ice skater doing a graceful **FIGURE-EIGHT TURN.**

NOT-SO-FUN FACT

Chicken pox can cause between 250 and 500 blisters on the human body!

TRUTH

Have you ever had chicken pox?

DARE

Pretend you are a famous photographer at a high-profile photo shoot.

Q. How should you photograph a water pitcher?

A. With *no filter*.

TRUTH

What food gives you the worst breath?

GRAY OR GREY?

What color is an elephant? Spell it! If you spelled it *G-R-A-Y*, you're right. You are using the more popular US spelling. If you spelled it *G-R-E-Y*, you're also right. This is the more popular spelling in the rest of the English-speaking world.

DARE

Stomp around on all fours like an ELEPHANT.

DID YOU KNOW?

Certain sports, like basketball, tennis, and running, can strengthen your bones.

TRUTH

Have you ever broken a bone?

DARE

Write a friend a note with missing letters and have them decode it.

The Rosetta stone is an ancient Egyptian stone inscribed with multiple languages and scripts. Thanks to this stone, we now understand a lot more about ancient languages and writings.

TRUTH

Have you ever fallen off your bike?

DID YOU KNOW?

One type of early bicycle, called the "penny-farthing," had a giant wheel in front and a small wheel in back.

Q. Why did the bicycle have so many friends?

A. It was well-rounded!

DARE

WEAR *a bicycle helmet for the next hour.*

Q. Why is the dog so grumpy?

A. She's having a *ruff* day.

TRUTH

If you were a dog, what kind of dog would you be?

DARE

Write *your and your crush's initials in a heart.*

DID YOU KNOW?

There are different theories about what originally inspired the heart shape; it may have been plant leaves, seed pods, human body parts, or something else entirely!

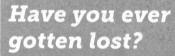

TRUTH

Have you ever gotten lost?

WHERE'S FIDO?

Dogs and cats can be microchipped so that they can be identified and safely returned home if they get lost. These microchips are very small—about the size of a grain of rice!

DARE

Pretend you're a football player scoring a _GAME-WINNING TOUCHDOWN_.

WHICH WAY IS UP?

M. C. Escher was a graphic artist who could depict staircases that looked like they were going both up and down at once.

TRUTH

Have you ever fallen down—or up—a staircase?

DARE

Draw a COMPLICATED MAZE and challenge a friend to solve it in less than one minute.

The largest permanent hedge maze in the world can be found in Yancheng, Jiangsu, China—the maze's pathway is over 30,000 feet long!

TRUTH

What was your last birthday wish?

Q. How was the candle's birthday party?

A. It was a huge blowout!

THAT'S A LOT OF WAX!

The world record for most lit candles on a birthday cake is 72,585! After the candles were extinguished, the wax had to be scraped off before the partygoers could eat the cake.

DARE

Pretend to blow out all the candles on a HUGE cake.

DID YOU KNOW?

Fainting is caused by a lack of blood flow to the brain.

TRUTH

Have you ever fainted?

210

DARE

Try to draw a MASTERPIECE in one minute and hang it on your wall.

Q. Why did the sculptor start over?

A. She wanted a clean *slate*.

TRUTH

What would you choose as your name if you could pick your own?

Q. How do knights like to be called?

A. By their *sir*-names.

SPEAKING OF ROCKS . . .

There is a mysterious stone circle monument in England known as Stonehenge. Who created it? Nobody can say for sure, but wild theories abound—one legend claims that Merlin the wizard built it!

DARE

Challenge a friend to a game of ROCK, PAPER, SCISSORS.

BETTER THAN AN ID TAG

A family in Japan taught their parrot, Yosuke, to say his full name and address in case he ever got lost. It was a good thing they did! Yosuke flew away one day, but was reunited with his family after he told a veterinarian who he was and where he lived.

TRUTH

What was the name of your first pet?

DARE

Lap milk out of a bowl on the floor LIKE A CAT.

Although lots of children's stories feature cats happily lapping up milk, many cats are actually lactose intolerant.

TRUTH

Who was your first crush?

Q. How did the web designers know they were meant to be web designers?

A. It was love at first *site*!

A 30-second Super Bowl commercial can cost more than 5 million dollars. Advertisers are willing to pay this amount for the chance to reach over 100 million viewers!

DARE

IMPROVISE a commercial for the first product you see.

TRUTH

Have you ever had overdue library books?

DARE

Turn a book UPSIDE DOWN and try to read a page aloud.

Some talented designers are able to design a word so that it reads the same both right-side up and upside down. This type of design is called an "ambigram," and it has been around for over 100 years!

TRUTH

Have you ever taken something from a hotel room?

DID YOU KNOW?

Over 4,000 hotels donate their customers' used soaps to an organization that repurposes them and provides new soap to those in need.

DON'T TRY THIS AT HOME

Some people are addicted to eating paper, including toilet paper! This condition is called "xylophagia."

DARE

Walk around with a piece of TOILET PAPER stuck to your shoe.

(Tip: A little water might help it stick.)

NOT-SO-SWEET DREAMS

If you've ever had a nightmare about being naked in public, you're not alone. This is just one of many common scary dreams. Others include falling, being unable to speak, and having your teeth fall out.

TRUTH

Have you ever dreamed that you went to school naked?

DARE

Show everyone your WORST school picture.

Q. How did the pencil get straight A's?

A. It was the *sharpest* in the class.

TRUTH

Would you go bungee jumping?

Q. Why are bungee jumpers so fearless?

A. They live life on the edge.

Q. Why was the cooking show host in a hurry?

A. She was running out of *thyme*.

DARE

Try a food you've NEVER EATEN before.
(But nothing dangerous! Check with an adult first to make sure it's okay.)

TRUTH

What is one thing you do when no one is looking?

DARE

Wear a FUNNY HAT for the rest of the day.
(If you don't have one, make one!)

A person who designs and makes hats is called a "milliner."

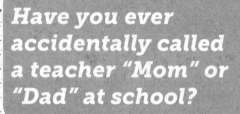

TRUTH

Have you ever accidentally called a teacher "Mom" or "Dad" at school?

DID YOU KNOW?

Teachers must often act *in loco parentis*, a Latin phrase that means "in the place of a parent."

Q. Why don't rats play basketball?

A. They are *sewer* losers.

DARE

Play SPORTS CHARADES with your friends—act out a sport, and see if they can guess it.

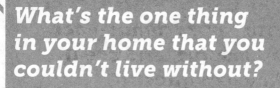

TRUTH

What's the one thing in your home that you couldn't live without?

DARE

Try to read your friend's MIND.

Don't have telepathic superpowers? Not to worry! You can learn a lot about what someone is thinking and feeling by paying attention to their body language and tone of voice.

TRUTH

Have you ever pretended a hairbrush was a microphone?

DID YOU KNOW?

It's normal to lose up to 100 hairs a day.

Cows have stomachs with 4 different chambers!

DARE

MOO like a cow.

TRUTH

What is your worst bad habit?

DARE

Pretend to be a WORLD-FAMOUS Hula-Hooper and show off some tricks.

Hoop Rolling is a game for children that involves rolling a hoop with a stick for as long as possible. Hoop games go as far back as ancient Greece and Rome!

TRUTH

Have you ever stepped in dog poop?

DID YOU KNOW?

Not all animal poop is undesirable! Manure contains animal feces, which is often used by farmers to fertilize their land.

FOLLOW THE NOSE

Police departments all over the world use bloodhounds to track the scent of missing persons.

DARE

SNIFF around the room like a bloodhound.

Shooting stars are actually meteors or meteoroids that have entered Earth's atmosphere.

TRUTH

Have you ever made a wish on a shooting star?

DARE

Play a DRUM SOLO.
(If you don't have drums, grab a stick and some boxes or buckets!)

In a traditional orchestra, there are four sections of instruments: woodwinds, brass, strings, and percussion (which includes drums).

TRUTH

Have you ever eaten food that fell on the ground?

MYTHBUSTER

The "5-second rule" won't protect you from getting sick!

To wish an actor or musician luck before a performance, say "Break a leg!" instead of "Good luck!"

DARE

Give a monologue like you are the star of a DRAMATIC PLAY.

The "Black Death" epidemic in the 14th century was caused by rodents carrying bacteria-infested fleas, which bit humans and made them sick! Luckily, we now have antibiotics to treat this type of infection.

TRUTH

Are you scared of rats or mice?

DARE

Pretend to be an all-powerful WIZARD.

(Tip: Grab something to use as a magical staff!)

Many of the spell names in the Harry Potter books are based on Latin words (lumos comes from the Latin *lumen*, which means "light").

TRUTH

If you could be invisible for a day, what would you do?

HEY, WHERE'D YOU GO?

Though not "invisible," there are several types of animals that are partially—or even mostly—transparent, including certain kinds of frogs, butterflies, and jellyfish.

DARE

Create your own yoga pose. BE CREATIVE!

DID YOU KNOW?
Over 100 million doses
of flu vaccine are distributed
each year!

TRUTH

*Have you ever pretended
to be sick to get out of
something?*

DARE

Come up with a SECRET handshake with a friend.

People all over the world greet one another in different ways— some hug, others bow to each other, and some kiss on both cheeks.

TRUTH

Are you scared of heights?

DID YOU KNOW?
Some skydivers jump from heights of 15,000 feet!

GORILLA GRUB

Gorillas are vegetarian! Gorilla species have different diets depending on where they live. Some gorillas like to eat leaves and shoots, while others prefer munching on fruit.

DARE

Beat your chest like a GORILLA.

Q. Why was the monster hiding under the bed?

A. He was scared of humans!

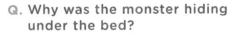

TRUTH

Have you ever checked under your bed for monsters?

DARE

Do your best "SNORT" laugh.

Q. Why was the boy quarantined?

A. His laughter was *infectious*!

TRUTH

Have you ever accidentally dropped a roll of toilet paper into the toilet?

Q. Why did the toilet need a break?

A. It was feeling *flushed*.

252

WATCH YOUR STEP!

Are you nimble on your feet? Laser rooms allow thrill-seekers to try venturing through a maze without activating a laser beam and setting off an alarm.

DARE

PRETEND to be walking across hot coals.

DID YOU KNOW?

The world's first electronic television was invented in 1927—and the inventor, Philo Taylor Farnsworth, was only 21 years old!

TRUTH

What TV show(s) are you embarrassed to love?

DARE

Put a TV show on MUTE and make up your own dialogue.

Q. Why was the remote control angry?

A. Everyone was always pushing its buttons!

TRUTH

Have you ever shared a secret you weren't supposed to share?

DID YOU KNOW?

To make sure that sensitive information doesn't fall into the wrong hands, confidential documents often contain type that is "redacted," or made unreadable. Redacted text is usually covered in thick black lines so it can't be seen.

Q. What did the clown's valentine say?

A. "Be *mime*."

DARE

Send someone a *VALENTINE*—*even if it's not Valentine's Day!*

TRUTH

Do you bite your nails?

DARE

Give a friend a
PEDICURE.

Humans aren't
the only ones
who can enjoy a
spa day. Dog spas
allow our furry friends
to get pampered with
services like baths,
massages, and even
"pawdicures."

TRUTH

What was the last thing you got in trouble for?

Q. Why did the salad get sent to her room?

A. She was being too *fresh*.

Q. Why did the dancer need a tissue?

A. He had a *boogie*.

DARE

Dance like a DISCO STAR.

(Tip: Don't know what disco is? Ask a grown-up who lived through the 1970s!)

SUPERSONIC!

If an aircraft "breaks the sound barrier," that means it's traveling faster than the speed of sound. This is called supersonic flight.

TRUTH

If you could fly anywhere in the world, where would you go?

DARE

Pretend you're a BASEBALL PLAYER hitting a home run.

Cal Ripken Jr. holds the record for most consecutive baseball games played—2,632 games!

TRUTH

Has your bathing suit ever fallen off while swimming?

Q. What do elephants wear to the watering hole?

A. Swim trunks!

MY LEFT OR YOUR LEFT?

In theater, "blocking" is the term for determining where performers move while onstage. Actors may be told by the director to go "stage right" or "stage left," which are opposite from what someone in the audience would see as right or left.

DARE

SING *your favorite show tune.*

TRUTH

Have you ever dropped a phone or computer?

DARE

Go the rest of the day *WITHOUT* using the internet.

Modern smartphones have more memory, storage space, and computing power than NASA's *Voyager* spacecrafts!

TRUTH

Have you ever been bitten by an animal?

DID YOU KNOW?

Rabies, which means "madness" in Latin, can cause humans to develop a fear of water.

DARE

HEE-HAW
like a donkey.

What do you call a soft drink? If you live in the US, you probably say *soda* or *pop*, but these carbonated beverages are called *fizzy drinks* in the UK.

TRUTH

Have you ever gotten a free refill when you weren't supposed to?

DARE

Conduct an _IMAGINARY_ orchestra.

The tool an orchestra conductor uses to lead the musicians is called a "baton" (though some conductors prefer to conduct with just their hands).

TRUTH

Do you wear deodorant?

DID YOU KNOW?

Perspiration is another word for "sweat."

Q. What kind of fish likes to make others laugh?

A. Clownfish!

DARE

Let a friend put *CLOWN MAKEUP* on your face.

BOVINE BURPS

Cows burp . . . a lot! In fact, burps from cows account for about 26% of methane gas emissions in the United States!

TRUTH

When was the last time you burped in public?

DARE

RUN in place as fast as you can for one minute.

A woman in the UK holds the record for the fastest marathon ever run— on stilts! Her time was 6 hours, 37 minutes, and 38 seconds.

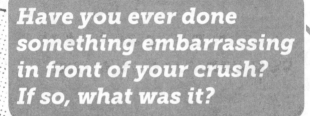

TRUTH

Have you ever done something embarrassing in front of your crush? If so, what was it?

Q. Why doesn't the bird like to eat caterpillars?

A. She doesn't want to get butterflies in her stomach.

Karaoke means "empty orchestra" in Japanese.

DARE

SING your favorite karaoke song.

During Victorian times, many children would only bathe once a week (if they were lucky enough to bathe at all).

TRUTH

How long have you gone without taking a shower or bath?

DARE

Challenge a friend to a NO-BLINKING contest.

Ever notice how some animals, like reptiles, appear to have a third eyelid on each eye? This is called a "nictitating membrane," and it helps protect their eyes.

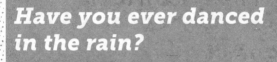

TRUTH

Have you ever danced in the rain?

FREEZING DESERT

It would be hard to dance in the rain in Antarctica—the continent gets so little rainfall that it's actually considered a desert despite all the ice and snow!

DARE

Do ten JUMPING JACKS.

Q. What did the ram say to the sheep?

A. "*Ewe* mean everything to me."

TRUTH

Who was the last person you said "I love you" to?

DARE

**SQUARE DANCE
with a friend.**

FUN FACT

The phrase
do-si-do comes
from the French
dos-à-dos, which
means "back-to-back."

TRUTH

Have you ever gotten locked out of your house?

A THIEF'S BEST FRIEND

A skeleton key is a key that can open many different locks because its serrated edge has been filed down.

Q. Why didn't the band play
   any country music?
A. They were in a city that day.

DARE

Make up your own
COUNTRY SONG.

TRUTH

Name one weird thing that you're afraid of.

DARE

Move around the room as *SLOWLY* as a sloth.

Sloths are the slowest-moving mammals in the world. They move so slowly that algae grows on their coats!

TRUTH

Have you ever wondered if your stuffed animals or action figures are alive?

DID YOU KNOW?

Kids have played with dolls for hundreds—possibly thousands—of years. Some dolls have been found that date back as far as 4 or 5 thousand years.

WHAT'S HIS NAME?

While many people think Frankenstein is the name of the monster, in the original novel by Mary Shelley, it was actually the name of the scientist who created him: Victor Frankenstein.

DARE

Act like you are **FRANKENSTEIN'S MONSTER** coming to life for the first time.

Q. Why did the girl play soccer?
A. She got a real *kick* out of it.

TRUTH

If you could be a professional athlete in any sport, what sport would it be?

DARE

Make your own MUSIC VIDEO.

FUN FACT

The first music video to play on MTV was "Video Killed the Radio Star" by the Buggles. The whole video was filmed in just one day.

TRUTH

Are you scared of thunderstorms?

STORM SCIENCE

You see lightning before you hear thunder because light travels faster than sound.

Eyebrow hairs have a life span of about four months—so all of the eyebrow hairs you had several months ago have probably fallen out and have been replaced by now!

DARE

Try to move only ONE EYEBROW at a time.

HEY, PAL!

A trick to correctly spelling the word "principal" is to remember it has the word "pal" in it.

TRUTH

Have you ever gotten sent to the principal's office?

DARE

Pretend to surf a
BIG WAVE.
(Be careful not to wipe out!)

In 2018,
a Brazilian
surfer in Portugal
broke a world
record by surfing
an 80-foot wave.

TRUTH

Have you ever broken a promise?

THE PROMISE KEEPER

Legend has it that when the Roman general Marcus Atilius Regulus was captured in war, his enemies allowed him to return home one last time— if he promised to return. Regulus agreed. He went home to speak with the Roman Senate and see his family. Then, true to his word, he returned to his captors.

One person's two feet aren't always the same size. In fact, some stores provide special options for people who need to buy shoes in different sizes.

DARE

Wear *TWO* DIFFERENT shoes for the rest of the day.

Q. Why didn't the young men want to go skiing?

A. They knew it would be all *downhill* from there.

TRUTH

What is the bravest thing you've ever done?

DARE

QUICK—make up a story about a daring adventure! You have one minute to think before you have to tell a friend.

DID YOU KNOW?

In 1937, world-famous aviator Amelia Earhart and her navigator, Fred Noonan, set out to fly around the world. During the journey, they mysteriously disappeared, and they were never heard from again.

TRUTH

How many US states have you been to?

DID YOU KNOW?

Passing through Arizona? Leave the cacti alone! Cutting down a saguaro cactus is against state law in Arizona because these cacti take so long to grow.

Q. What was the man doing when he skinned his knee?

A. He was on a road *trip*.

DARE

See how many **US** states you can name in one minute.

DON'T SNORE—SING!

A choir director in the UK has developed a singing course that may help reduce snoring.

TRUTH

Do you snore?

DARE

Pretend you've just WON THE LOTTERY!

In 2016, a lottery jackpot reached a whopping $1,586,400,000, setting a record for the greatest jackpot in a national lottery!

TRUTH

Have you ever forgotten a friend's birthday?

DID YOU KNOW?

September is the most common birth month.

HAHA!

Ever heard that laughter is the best medicine? Turns out laughing *is* good for you! Laughing can reduce stress and boost your immune system.

DARE

Do one minute of stand-up COMEDY.

Q. How did the internet star find out about her surprise party?

A. She saw all the *streamers*.

TRUTH

What were the last good and bad surprises you got?

DARE

Try NOT to use any electricity or electronic devices for the next twenty minutes.

Q. Why can't comedians tell jokes about electricity?

A. The jokes are too *shocking*.

TRUTH

If you won a million dollars, what would you buy?

BREAK THE BANK

A million dollars is a lot of money, but it's not enough to buy a private jet. Private jets start at around two million dollars, but some cost more than a hundred million!

DARE

Make up a TONGUE TWISTER and say it three times fast.

(Or use this one: "Sally sells seashells by the seashore.")

TRUTH

Would you rather go scuba diving or sky diving?

DARE

Keep your eyes closed for three minutes. NO PEEKING!

Earthworms don't have eyes. They rely on light receptors to tell them where to go (or where not to go—they prefer the dark).

TRUTH

Have you ever thrown up in public?

FUN FACT

American inventor Gilmore Schjeldahl was the creator of the modern airsickness bag (more commonly known as the "barf bag").

There are laws preventing people in most areas from adopting unusual pets, but some organizations allow you to symbolically adopt wild animals to help protect them in their natural habitats.

DARE

Ask your parent or guardian if you can adopt an **UNUSUAL ANIMAL**, like an emu, panda, or narwhal, and see what they say!

WHADDAYACALLEM?

Before men wore pants, they wore other two-legged garments with funny names like pantaloons, knickerbockers, and breeches.

TRUTH

Have you ever torn a pair of pants you were wearing?

DARE

POSE *like a mannequin at the mall.*

Q. What did one crash dummy say to the other?

A. "*Mannequin* wait to go home!"

TRUTH

Do you ever chew with your mouth open?

Q. What is the saddest cheese of all?

A. *Blue* cheese.

Many brilliant minds throughout history have recorded their thoughts and theories in notebooks, including Thomas Edison, Marie Curie, and Leonardo da Vinci!

DARE

Read a page of your journal or diary **OUT LOUD**.

TRUTH

Have you ever eavesdropped on a conversation?

DARE

Play *AIR GUITAR*.

Air guitar
fans are
able to show
their shredding
skills in actual
competitions, such
as the Air Guitar World
Championships.

TRUTH

Have you ever returned (or regifted) a present from someone?

DID YOU KNOW?

The Statue of Liberty was a gift from France to the United States in 1886. Good thing the United States didn't regift it—it's become a national icon!

Q. How did the girl win the arm-wrestling match?

A. She was able to get the upper hand.

DARE

ARM WRESTLE *a friend.*

TRUTH

Have you ever used an outhouse?

DARE

Challenge a friend to a *DANCE-OFF*.

Q. What type of dance is most popular in the forest?

A. The *fox*-trot.

TRUTH

Have you ever lied about your age?

DID YOU KNOW?

People born on February 29 during a leap year are called "leaplings," and they only get to celebrate their birthday on its actual date once every four years. So a leapling born 12 years ago might have only had 3 real birthdays!

DARE

NEIGH like a horse.

DID YOU KNOW?

Inventor Thomas Edison, who is responsible for many advancements in lighting, held over 1,093 patents!

TRUTH

Do you sleep with a night-light?

DARE

PRETEND *you are walking on a tightrope.*

In 1859,
a French
acrobat crossed
Niagara Falls on a
tightrope.

TRUTH

Are you scared of speaking in front of a crowd?

Q. What was the mouse's biggest fear?
A. Public *squeaking*!

DARE

WHISTLE a tune and have a friend guess the song.

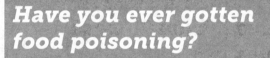

TRUTH

Have you ever gotten food poisoning?

DARE

Give an _IMPROMPTU SPEECH_ about your favorite food.

A common red food dye called carmine is made from ground-up bugs. Yum!

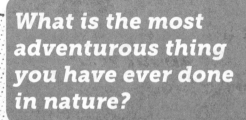

TRUTH

What is the most adventurous thing you have ever done in nature?

DID YOU KNOW?

Mount Everest, the highest point on earth, is named after Sir George Everest, a British surveyor.

Q. Where do wrestlers learn new tricks?

A. In their *weight class*!

DARE

Pretend you are a PROFESSIONAL BODYBUILDER posing for pictures.

Saltwater crocodiles weigh 1,000 pounds on average. Some weigh twice as much—or more!

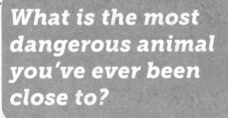

TRUTH

What is the most dangerous animal you've ever been close to?

DARE

Have a conversation with a friend in a MADE-UP LANGUAGE.

A *polyglot* is a person who knows several different languages.

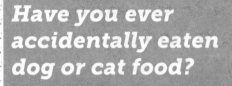

TRUTH

Have you ever accidentally eaten dog or cat food?

DID YOU KNOW?

Some restaurants offer menus specifically for customers' dogs. These menus include a wide variety of options, from farm-to-table fare to casual comfort food to—of course—strips of bacon!

DARE

DANCE like you're at a rock concert.

Q. Why did the man stand on a clock?

A. He wanted to be on time.

TRUTH

If you had a time machine, when would you travel to?

DARE

Stand COMPLETELY STILL for one minute.

DON'T MOVE!

Street performers who dress up like statues and pose for long periods of time are called "living statues." Sometimes they blend in so well, people walking by think they are really statues!

339

TRUTH

Have you ever written a poem or a song?

Q. Why are porcupines such good writers?

A. They have so many quills!

A lot of bacteria live in your armpits! In fact, body odor is the result of those bacteria breaking down the proteins in your sweat.

DARE

SMELL *your armpit.*

Legend has it that George Washington cut down a cherry tree when he was a kid. When confronted by his father, George said, "I cannot tell a lie" and admitted to the deed. But this story about honesty was completely made up by a biographer!

TRUTH

Have you ever told a lie to get out of trouble?

DARE

Tell a SCARY STORY to a friend.

Scary stories often begin with "It was a dark and stormy night . . ." but do you know where this line came from? It first appeared as the opening line in the novel *Paul Clifford* by Edward Bulwer-Lytton (1830).

343

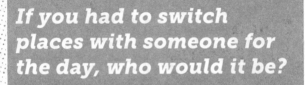

TRUTH

If you had to switch places with someone for the day, who would it be?

DID YOU KNOW?

There are lots of Elvis Presley impersonators all over the world. These impersonators often participate in festivals and contests celebrating the "King of Rock and Roll."

Q. How did the pizza delivery man propose?

A. With a doorbell ring.

DARE

Call someone and tell them a CHEESY joke.

TRUTH

Have you ever gotten carsick?

DARE

Pretend you are a ZOMBIE hungry for brains.

Q. What do you call undead bugs that love honey?

A. Zom-*bees*!

TRUTH

Have you ever gotten diarrhea at someone else's house?

POOP TO THE RESCUE

You've probably heard of organ transplants, but have you heard of fecal transplants? Scientists are currently studying whether stool (poop) transplants can help patients with certain medical conditions.

DID YOU KNOW?

Why are sneakers called sneakers? The name refers to how the rubber soles allow people to walk (or *sneak*) around noiselessly.

DARE

SWITCH SHOES with a friend for the next hour.

TRUTH

What song do you know all of the words to by heart?

DARE

BARK like a dog.

Q. Why did the beagle climb the stairs?

A. He wanted to be top dog.

TRUTH

Have you ever spilled something on your clothes in public?

Q. Why wasn't the magician upset about the ink spill on her clothes?

A. It was invisible ink!

While the American pronunciation for the letter Z is "zee," the British pronunciation is "zed."

DARE

Recite the alphabet BACKWARDS from Z to A.

Q. How was the elevator's day?

A. It had its ups and downs.

TRUTH

Have you ever gotten stuck in an elevator?

DARE

Put together your CRAZIEST OUTFIT.

Q. Why did the model go to the airport?

A. He was a *runway* model.

TRUTH

What is one thing that always annoys you?

IT'S DRIVING ME NUTS!

A "pet peeve" is something that really gets on your nerves. Common pet peeves include loud chewing, excessive horn honking, and toenail clipping in public.

DID YOU KNOW?

About 45 million turkeys are eaten in the US every Thanksgiving!

DARE

GOBBLE like a turkey.

FUN FACT

The largest pizza ever made was in Italy and spanned over 13,500 square feet!

TRUTH

Can you eat a whole pizza in one sitting?

DARE

Eat a *SPOONFUL* of ketchup.

Ketchup is very popular in America! In fact, 97% of American households say they have ketchup in their kitchens.

TRUTH

If you could be any animal, what would you be?

DID YOU KNOW?

A *phoenix* is a mythical bird that is reborn out of the ashes of fire.

FUN FACT

Pigs roll around in mud to help stay cool in the heat. This is called "wallowing."

DARE

OINK *like a pig.*

TRUTH

Have you ever intentionally eaten someone else's food?

DARE

PRETEND to itch like you are covered in a rash.

Taking a bath with oatmeal can help relieve itching from poison ivy.

TRUTH

If you could be any type of famous performer, what would you be?

DID YOU KNOW?

In the entertainment industry, a person who can sing, dance, and act is known as a "triple threat."

DARE

Try to J U G G L E.

TRUTH

Are you scared of flying in an airplane?

DARE

SLITHER around like a snake.

Scientists have learned that snakes have a slick coating on their scales that helps them slither around more easily.

TRUTH

Who do you call the most?

FUN FACT

The largest telephone conference call ever included over 16,000 people.

DARE

Hold your nose and tell a funny story.

Q. Why did the actor bring her cell phone onstage?

A. She needed to make a *curtain call*.

TRUTH

Do you have stage fright?

DARE

Tie your shoes with only ONE HAND.

DID YOU KNOW?

The hard end of a shoelace actually has a name—it's called an "aglet."

TRUTH

Have you ever taken more than one free sample from a shop or grocery store?

Q. What is a rabbit's favorite dessert?
A. Carrot cake.

In the wild, wolves use howls as a way of communicating with each other.

DARE

HOWL like a wolf.

700 AND COUNTING

Scientists have discovered about 700 dinosaur species so far—but they believe there are many more still to be discovered.

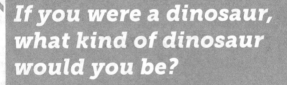

TRUTH

If you were a dinosaur, what kind of dinosaur would you be?

DARE

Act like a _T. rex_ with _tiny arms_.

T. rex fossils have been found in the Northwestern United States, including Montana and South Dakota!

TRUTH

Who knows the most about you?

Q. What do mermaids tell their best friends?

A. *Sea*-crets.

Q. What kind of horse is nocturnal?

A. A *night*-mare!

DARE

Describe your SCARIEST DREAM.

TRUTH

What was your most embarrassing moment in gym class?

Do AS MANY push-ups as you can.

Q. Why did the bodybuilder quit the competition?

A. It wasn't worth the *weight*.

TRUTH

Have you ever accidentally walked into a door or wall?

DID YOU KNOW?

Safety glass is a special type of glass that's designed to break into small pieces when broken, causing less harm than large, jagged pieces.

Q. Why did the rabbit go to the store?

A. He needed to go grocery *hopping*.

DARE

HOP on one foot all the way across the room without falling over.

TRUTH

Do you ever wish you were a twin or a triplet?

DARE

Write a poem about someone you love.

Petrarch, a famous Italian poet, wrote more than 300 sonnets to his beloved "Laura" (though critics don't necessarily agree on who Laura was, or if she was a real person at all).

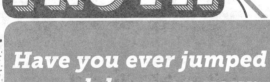

TRUTH

Have you ever jumped up and down on your bed?

DID YOU KNOW?

The "Do Not Remove" tags on mattresses are for mattress sellers, not their customers.

Apes are able to laugh like humans. In fact, research suggests they might even be ticklish.

DARE

*Try to **FROWN** for one minute straight while a friend tries to make you laugh.*

DID YOU KNOW?

Slippery, wet conditions can cause cars to *hydroplane*, which means they lose contact with the roadway and start skidding!

TRUTH

Have you ever been sprayed with water by a passing car?

DARE

Do a SPIT TAKE like a comedy actor.
(A spit take is when an actor spits out water in astonishment or surprise.)

Spit takes made quite a *splash* on television in the 1950s, especially on *The Danny Thomas Show*.

TRUTH

Have you ever talked a babysitter into letting you stay up late?

FUN FACT

The longest that a human has voluntarily stayed awake is 264 hours. Randy Gardner performed this feat in 1964 when he was 17 years old for a science experiment he was conducting with a friend.

All house cats are the same species, though there are many different breeds.

DARE

MEOW like a cat.

DID YOU KNOW?

An inventor received a US patent in 1868 for a coffin that could allow a buried person to indicate that they were still alive by ringing a bell!

TRUTH

Are you scared of graveyards?

DARE

BUZZ around like a bumblebee.

Q. Why did the bee go to the doctor?

A. She had *hives*.

TRUTH

What song most reminds you of your crush?

DID YOU KNOW?

There are dozens of songs with "I Love You" as the title (and even more if you include different spellings).

DARE

Talk like a `robot` **for the next five minutes.**

Q. Why don't noses mind being sorted onto teams?

A. They are likely to get picked!

TRUTH

Have you ever been picked last for a team?

DARE

Make FUNNY FACES in the mirror for as long as you can without laughing.

FUN FACT

Engineers in the Norwegian town of Rjukan figured out a way to use giant mirrors to reflect sunlight onto their shade-covered village.

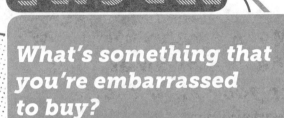

TRUTH

What's something that you're embarrassed to buy?

THE TELLTALE SIGNS

How can you tell if someone is embarrassed? Often, embarrassment causes people to blush, look down, turn their head away, or touch their face.

DARE

Use a parrot voice to COPY EVERYTHING your friends or family say for the next minute.

Q. What's the most powerful sandwich of all?

A. The hero!

TRUTH

If you were a superhero, what kind would you be?

DARE

Give yourself a **SUPERHERO** name and have your friends and family call you by it for the rest of the day.

Q. What kind of bad guy likes to ruin your dinner?

A. A *supper*-villain!

TRUTH

What is your best hide-and-seek hiding spot?

FUN FACT

The biggest game of hide-and-seek ever played was in Chengdu, China, in 2014. Over 1,400 people played at once!

Q. Why didn't the actor take the mime job?

A. She didn't want to get boxed in.

DARE

Act like a MIME trapped inside a glass box.

TRUTH

What is your deepest, darkest secret?

DARE

Come up with YOUR OWN TRUTH OR DARE to ask your friends!

In movies, anyone who takes a "truth serum" is forced to tell the truth. In real life, however, no magically effective truth serum actually exists.